The Power and Purpose of Preaching in the Christian Faith

The Power and Purpose of Preaching in the Christian Faith

Baffour Nkrumah-Appiah, (Rev.)

Baffour Nkrumah-Appiah, (Rev.)
The Power and Purpose of Preaching in the Christian Faith

Published by Spines
ISBN 979-8-89569-854-9

Contents

Dedicated

To

The men and women whom the Lord has called to bring His message of salvation into a lost world

and

My family

Christiana Nkrumah-Appiah

Alexander Nkrumah-Appiah

William Nkrumah-Appiah

Jane Okeke Adedamola

Barry Adedamola

Introduction

Preaching is not merely the sharing of words:

It is the proclamation of the Gospel—the good news of Jesus Christ—and the living out of God's Word in a community of faith. Through preaching, the Church connects its members to the transforming power of Scripture, invites them into deeper intimacy with God, and equips them for the mission of the Kingdom of God.

This collection of sermons represents a journey into the heart of Christian doctrine, the mysteries of the faith, and the practical outworking of biblical truths in our everyday lives. As you engage with this series, you will encounter a rich collection of themes, each sermon building upon the next, offering a comprehensive exploration of the Christian faith.

The Theological Significance of Preaching:

In the Christian tradition, preaching has always held a central place. It is through preaching that the Word of God is proclaimed and made known to the world. The Apostle Paul, in Romans 10:14-15, famously declares, "How then can they call on the one they have not believed in? And how can they believe in the one of whom they have not heard? And how can they hear without someone preaching to them? And how can anyone preach unless they are sent?" These verses highlight the essential role of preaching in bringing the Gospel to the world.

The act of preaching is not only an academic exercise but a divine calling and a means of grace through which God speaks to His people. Historically, Christian preaching has been seen as a crucial means by which God's truth is communicated. From the early Church Fathers to the Reformation preachers like Martin Luther and John Calvin, preaching has served as a tool for the purification and edification of the Church. In the present day, preaching continues to be a vital channel for conveying doctrinal truths, providing spiritual nourishment, and calling individuals to discipleship.

The Structure of This Sermon Series:

This sermon collection aims to offer a comprehensive exploration of the Christian faith from several perspectives. Each sermon addresses a different facet of our relationship with God, our identity in Christ, and our calling as believers in the world. The topics selected for this series reflect the timeless truths of Scripture, the relevance of the Gospel for modern life, and the ways in which the Christian message speaks to the deep needs of the human heart.

The series is divided into several thematic sections, each focusing on a particular aspect of Christian belief and practice. Some of the key themes explored in this collection include:

1. The Nature of God: Understanding who God is—His attributes, His sovereignty, and His relational nature.

2. Salvation and the Cross: Exploring the central event of the Christian faith—the death and resurrection of Jesus Christ—and what it means for believers today.
3. Living the Christian Life: Practical applications of the Gospel, including themes of holiness, obedience, and discipleship.
4. The Church and the Kingdom of God: The role of the Church in the world, the importance of community, and the mission of God's people.
5. The End Times and Eternal Hope: A look at the ultimate hope for believers, the return of Christ, and the promise of eternal life.

Each sermon has been carefully crafted to speak to both the intellectual and spiritual needs of the listener. They are grounded in Scripture, rich with theological reflection, and designed to inspire personal transformation. Whether you are a new believer or a seasoned disciple, these messages will challenge, encourage, and equip you to live more fully for the glory of God.

Chapter 1

Message: Four Days Late, He's Still On Time

Scripture: John 11:38-43

Introduction:

Question? Has there been a time when it seems like Jesus is late in your life? At the end of this message, you will be convinced that His timing is always perfect.

Our anchor for this message comes from the Gospel of John, chapter 11, verses 38-43, where we witness the powerful resurrection of Lazarus.

Join me then as we dig into this passage and explore other related scriptures as we try to understand this timeless message that Jesus is never late; He is always on time.

Turn with me into Scriptures.

Jesus Raises Lazarus From the Dead John 11:38-43

38 Jesus, once more deeply moved, came to the tomb. It was a cave with a stone laid across the entrance.

39 "Take away the stone," he said.

"But, Lord," said Martha, the sister of the dead man, "by this time there is a bad odor, for he has been there four days."

40 Then Jesus said, "Did I not tell you that if you believe, you will see the glory of God?"

41 So they took away the stone.

Then Jesus looked up and said, "Father, I thank you that you have heard me.

42 I knew that you always hear me, but I said this for the benefit of the people standing here, that they may believe that you sent me."

43 When he had said this, Jesus called in a loud voice, "Lazarus, come out!"

44 The dead man came out, his hands and feet wrapped with strips of linen, and a cloth around his face. Jesus said to them, "Take off the grave clothes and let him go."

So, what are the Narratives: In John 11:1-3, we encounter the story of Lazarus, a dear friend of Jesus, falling gravely ill.

Despite receiving the message of Lazarus' sickness, Jesus intentionally delays his arrival by four days. This delay becomes a powerful testament to the divine timing of Jesus.

The narrative unfolds to reveal that Jesus's apparent tardiness was a deliberate act to showcase the glory of God.

In waiting those extra days, Jesus intended to demonstrate that even when circumstances seem dire, and prayers seemingly go unanswered, God's timing is always perfect.

In verses 11:38-43, we witness the culmination of this divine plan as Jesus arrives at the tomb of Lazarus, where the mourners are grieving.

Amidst the sorrow, Jesus commands the stone covering the tomb to be rolled away, defying the expectations of those present.

In a moment that transcends human understanding, Jesus calls Lazarus forth, restoring him to life. This miraculous event serves as a profound reminder that God's timing is impeccable, and His ability to bring life out of death is beyond our comprehension.

The delay in Jesus' arrival wasn't a sign of neglect, but a deliberate orchestration of divine timing to manifest a miraculous resurrection, emphasizing the truth that even when we feel God is late, He is, in fact, perfectly on time.

1. Setting the Scene:

John 11:1-3 In the town of Bethany, a family experiences the sorrow of losing a loved one. Mary and Martha sent word to Jesus, saying, "Lord, the one you love is sick."

In our own lives, we often find ourselves in situations where we cry out to Jesus in the midst of our trials, feeling like He may be delayed in responding to our pleas.

2. Jesus' Delay:

(John 11:6): Surprisingly, upon hearing about Lazarus' illness, Jesus intentionally delays His arrival.

The scripture says, "So when he heard that Lazarus was sick, he stayed where he was two more days." This delay may seem puzzling, but it sets the stage for a profound revelation of God's glory.

Remember Church? I have consistently reminded you there was no event that took place in Jesus' walk on earth that was not pre-planned in the heavens. You see, Church, this was no different.

Why will you delay when your friend is in need, especially if we can help...isn't what the bible says we should do? So why did Jesus delay? Well, let us go on to read the bible.

3. The Divine Purpose:

John 11:4 Jesus declares, "This sickness will not end in death. No, it is for God's glory so that God's Son may be glorified through it.

Even in the face of what seems like a delay, there is a divine purpose at work. God's glory is about to be manifested in a way that will surpass human understanding.

Sometimes, we need to look beyond our physical surroundings, beyond constantly borrowing from the cousin, brother, sister who, by the way, doesn't keep your business to themselves but shares it with whoever asks them about your business.

Do you believe in Divine purpose? The Bible says, "Psalm 139:16- You saw me before I was born. Every day of my life was recorded in your book. Every moment was laid out before a single day had passed."

4. The Resurrection Power (John 11:38-43):

As Jesus finally arrives at the tomb of Lazarus, the atmosphere is thick with grief. Martha expresses her concern about the stench of death, as Lazarus has been dead for four days.

Yet, Jesus reassures her, saying, "Did I not tell you that if you believe, you will see the glory of God?" With unwavering faith, Jesus calls Lazarus out of the tomb, and the dead man comes out, bound hand and foot with linen strips. Yes, the delay is transformed into a powerful display of God's resurrection power.

5. Related Scriptures:

(Ecclesiastes 3:11) - "He has made everything beautiful in its time." God's timing is perfect, and He makes all things beautiful in His time.

Psalm 27:14 - "Wait for the LORD; be strong and take heart and wait for the LORD." Patience in waiting on the Lord leads to His perfect timing.

Isaiah 55:8-9 - "For my thoughts are not your thoughts, neither are your ways my ways." God's ways and timing surpass our understanding.

Conclusion:

In our lives, there will be moments when we feel like Jesus is four days late, but let us remember that He is still on time.

His delay serves a purpose, and in the waiting, His glory is revealed. May we trust in the resurrection power of Jesus, knowing that His timing is perfect, and He is always on time to bring life to the dead places in our lives. Amen.

Chapter 2
Message: Seeking God's Presence

Scripture Reading: Psalm 27:8 (NIV)

Psalm 27:8 says, "My heart says of you, 'Seek his face!' Your face, Lord, I will seek." This verse reflects a deep, heartfelt desire for communion with God.

The psalmist's invitation to seek God's face is an expression of longing for intimate fellowship with the Creator. Seeking God's presence is not simply about seeking answers or blessings, but about desiring to draw near to God in a personal and transformative way.

In ancient Israel, the "face" of God symbolized His presence and favor. The desire to seek His face implies a yearning for both His guidance and His nearness, which is a theme echoed throughout Scripture.

Seeking God's face, or His presence, is an essential aspect of the believer's spiritual life. It signifies an earnest pursuit of a relationship with God, not just through external acts of worship, but through an internal, personal longing for His nearness.

In Exodus 33:14, God promises Moses, "My presence will go with you, and I will give you rest." This shows that God's presence is not only a source of comfort but also of direction. When we seek God's face, we are essentially desiring to be in a place of peace and security, guided by His presence in all aspects of our lives.

In the New Testament, Jesus emphasizes the importance of seeking God's presence in the Sermon on the Mount, particularly in Matthew 7:7, where He says, "Ask and it will be given to you; seek and you will find; knock and the door will be opened to you."

This passage highlights the importance of persistent pursuit in the life of a disciple. Just as a child seeks out their parent for guidance and help, so too are believers called to seek God earnestly.

However, seeking God is not a one-time effort but a continual process of drawing near to Him, trusting that He will reveal Himself in His perfect timing. The psalmist's declaration in Psalm 27:8 reflects an understanding of the need for God's presence to guide and sustain him.

In Psalm 42:1-2, the psalmist expresses a similar desire, "As the deer pants for streams of water, so my soul pants for you, my God.

My soul thirsts for God, for the living God. When can I go and meet with God?" This metaphor of thirsting for God reinforces the deep spiritual longing that believers should feel for God's presence. Just as the body needs water to survive, the soul needs God's presence to thrive.

Finally, the invitation to seek God's face in Psalm 27:8 is not just for personal benefit but also for the greater purpose of glorifying God. As believers seek His presence, they are transformed into His image.

In 2 Corinthians 3:18, Paul writes, "And we all, who with unveiled faces contemplate the Lord's glory, are being transformed into His image with ever-increasing glory, which comes from the Lord, who is the Spirit."

The more we seek God's face, the more we are shaped by His character and nature. Seeking God's presence is not just a personal pursuit; it is also a way of reflecting His glory in the world.

In the end, the act of seeking God's face is an invitation to be changed, to be made more like Him, and to experience the fullness of joy that comes from His presence.

Chapter 3
Message: Victory over the vices of the enemy

Scripture: Ephesians 6:10-18

Victory over the vices of the enemy is not merely a distant hope but a present reality for every believer in Christ. Ephesians 6:10-18 points out the spiritual armor provided by God, which equips us to stand against the devil's schemes.

This passage reminds us that our battle is not against flesh and blood but against spiritual forces of wickedness in the heavenly places.

Each piece of these armors—the belt of truth, the breastplate of righteousness, the shoes of the gospel of peace, the shield of faith, the helmet of salvation, and the sword of the Spirit—serves as defense and offense in our spiritual warfare.

Wearing this armor daily, we fortify ourselves against the vices and temptations that seek to ensnare us, enabling us to resist and overcome them through the strength and power of God.

Psalm 149 also underscores the role of praise and worship in our victory over the enemy's vices. Verse 6 exhorts us to let the high praises of God be in our mouths and a two-edged sword in our hands.

This imagery vividly portrays praise as a weapon of spiritual warfare—a powerful tool that confounds the enemy and releases God's authority and presence into our circumstances.

As we lift our voices in worship and adoration, we align ourselves with God's purposes and declare His sovereignty over every situation. It speaks of executing judgment upon the enemy and binding their kings with chains—a testament to the authority and victory we have in Christ.

Combining these Scriptures, Ephesians 6:10-18 and Psalm 149, we find a comprehensive strategy for achieving victory over the vices of the enemy. The spiritual armor protects us from the attacks while empowering us to stand firm in God's truth and righteousness.

Additionally, praise becomes a weapon that dismantles strongholds and releases God's justice and authority. As believers, we are called to walk in this victory daily, knowing that through Christ, we are more than conquerors.

Jesus has already secured for us a victory, demonstrating His power to transform lives and bringing forth His kingdom on earth as it is in heaven.

Chapter 4

Message: Grace in a Troubled World

(A Sermon of Hope and Compassion)

Scripture: Ephesians 2:8

Right now, as we gather here, we are in the midst of a world fraught with conflict and turmoil. So, we gather here wondering when will it stop?

But we also want to understand, seeking, and hoping for grace. Our hearts ache as we witness the pain and suffering of our fellow human beings in various corners of the globe – in Israel and Gaza, in Russia and Ukraine, in Sudan, Haiti, and beyond.

However, we also gather not only to seek comfort and understanding in the midst of a troubled world, but also to reflect on how we can translate the universal principles of grace, hope, and compassion into tangible actions within our own local communities.

As we contemplate the global challenges facing humanity, let us remember that change begins at home, in the everyday interactions and choices that shape the world around us.

It is in times like these that we must turn to the eternal wisdom and boundless compassion of our Creator, finding comfort and guidance in the sacred texts that have illuminated the path of countless souls throughout the ages.

In the book of Micah, chapter 6, verse 8, we are reminded of what is required of us:

"He has told you, O mortal, what is good; and what does the Lord require of you but to do justice, and to love kindness, and to walk humbly with your God?"

So, we are not without instructions and guidance. These words resonate deeply with the essence of grace – to extend kindness and mercy to others, to advocate for justice and righteousness, and to walk in humility before our Creator.

Friends, the concept of grace is central to Christianity, it is the unmerited favor and love bestowed upon us by God.

You see, grace is the divine force that sustains us in times of trial, that uplifts us when we stumble, and that empowers us to extend kindness and mercy to others, even in the face of adversity.

In the book of Ephesians, chapter 2, verse 8, we are reminded: "For by grace you have been saved through faith. And this is not your own doing; it is the gift of God."

As we look to the troubled regions of our world, let us ask ourselves: How can we embody the spirit of grace within our own communities?

How can we be agents of hope and compassion in the face of adversity?

One way we can bring grace into our local communities is by fostering a culture of empathy and understanding.

In a world that is increasingly polarized and divided, let us strive to see beyond our differences and recognize the inherent dignity and worth of every individual.

This means listening with an open heart to those whose experiences may differ from our own and seeking common ground rather than dwelling on division.

Another way we can manifest grace in our communities is by actively engaging in acts of service and compassion.

Whether it's volunteering at a local food bank, reaching out to those who are marginalized or vulnerable, or simply offering a kind word or gesture to someone in need, each act of kindness has the power to ripple outward, creating a more compassionate and caring society.

Furthermore, let us not underestimate the power of community-building and solidarity in times of crisis.

Just as we stand in solidarity with our brothers and sisters around the world who are suffering, let us also come together as a community to support one another through life's challenges.

Whether it's organizing a neighborhood watch program to ensure safety and security or creating a support network for those struggling with mental health issues, there are countless ways we can extend grace to those around us.

As we contemplate the state of our world today, we should also reflect on how we can embody the spirit of grace in our thoughts, words, and deeds.

We should also look to the example set forth by Jesus Christ, who, in the face of persecution and injustice, preached a message of love, forgiveness, and reconciliation.

In the current events unfolding in Israel and Gaza, we see the devastating toll of violence and conflict.

Brothers and sisters, let us remember the words of Jesus from the Gospel of Matthew, chapter 5, verses 9-10: "Blessed are the peacemakers, for they will be called children of God.

As followers of Christ, we are called to be instruments of peace in a world torn apart by hatred and division.

And then, the ongoing tensions between Russia and Ukraine, let us heed the teachings of Jesus to love our enemies and pray for those who persecute us.

But most importantly, all of us should strive to see the humanity in all people, even those with whom we may vehemently disagree.

For it is only through understanding and compassion that lasting peace can be achieved.

And in Africa, especially in Sudan, where countless lives have been upended by political instability and humanitarian crises, let us not turn a blind eye to the suffering of our brothers and sisters.

Instead, let us extend a hand of solidarity and support, embodying the spirit of grace in our actions as we work towards a more just and equitable world for all.

Church, I am reminded by my wise spouse every day that the church is the light of the world, and in the face of seemingly unbelievable challenges, let us take comfort in the knowledge that grace abounds, even in the darkest of times.

We should always draw strength from the wellspring of divine love that flows unceasingly, nurturing and sustaining us through every trial and tribulation.

As we go forth from this place today, may we be beacons of hope and agents of grace in a troubled world.

May we seek peace where there is conflict, healing where there is pain, and love where there is hatred.

Let us be beacons of light in a world that often feels dark and uncertain, illuminating the path toward a brighter, more hopeful future for all.

And may the grace of our Lord Jesus Christ empower us to be instruments of positive change wherever we go. Amen.

Understanding Grace in Turbulent Times.

- Introduction: Defining grace and its significance in our lives.
- The Human Condition: Exploring the brokenness of the world.
- God's Unconditional Love: Reflecting on passages like Ephesians 2:8-9 and Romans 5:8.
- Grace in Action: Examples from the Bible (e.g., the story of the prodigal son in Luke 15:11-32).
- The Call to Extend Grace: Encouraging listeners to embody grace in their interactions.
- Conclusion: Finding hope in God's enduring grace amidst life's challenges.

Grace: The Antidote to Fear and Anxiety.

- Introduction: Acknowledging the prevalence of fear and anxiety in troubled times.
- The Promise of Peace: Scriptures such as Philippians 4:6-7 and John 14:27.
- Grace Overcomes Fear: Reflecting on Jesus' calming of the storm in Mark 4:35-41.
- Embracing God's Provision: Trusting in His grace to sustain us.
- Letting Go of Control: Surrendering our worries to God's grace.
- Conclusion: Encouraging listeners to find solace in God's grace amidst life's uncertainties.

The Transformative Power of Grace.

- Introduction: Highlighting the transformative nature of grace.
- From Brokenness to Wholeness: Exploring stories of transformation like Saul to Paul (Acts 9:1-22).
- Grace for All: Emphasizing God's inclusive love (Romans 3:23-24).
- Grace in Community: Building each other up in grace (Hebrews 10:24-25).
- Living Gracefully: Practicing forgiveness, compassion, and reconciliation.
- Conclusion: Encouraging listeners to embrace the transformative power of God's grace in their lives.

Grace: The Foundation of Christian Ethics.

- Introduction: Discussing the role of grace in shaping our moral compass.
- God's Grace and Justice: Examining passages like Micah 6:8 and Matthew 23:23.
- Extending Grace to Others: Learning from Jesus' example (John 8:1-11).
- Compassion in Action: Serving others with grace and humility (Matthew 25:35-40).
- Grace-Based Living: Integrating grace into our daily decisions and interactions.
- Conclusion: Challenging listeners to prioritize grace in their ethical framework.

Grace in Times of Suffering and Pain.

- Introduction: Acknowledging the reality of suffering in a troubled world.
- The Comfort of God's Presence: Scriptures such as Psalm 23:4 and Isaiah 43:2.
- Grace in Grief: Finding solace in God's grace during times of loss (2 Corinthians 1:3-4).
- Redemptive Suffering: Reflecting on the meaning of suffering in light of Christ's sacrifice (1 Peter 4:12-13).
- Sharing Burdens: Supporting one another with grace and compassion (Galatians 6:2).
- Conclusion: Encouraging listeners to lean on God's grace for strength and comfort in times of trial.

Embodying Grace in a Divided World.

- Introduction: Addressing the challenges of division and polarization.
- The Call to Unity: Scriptures such as Ephesians 4:3 and Colossians 3:14.
- Grace-Based Reconciliation: Learning from Jesus' teachings on forgiveness (Matthew 18:21-22).
- Breaking Down Barriers: Overcoming prejudice and discrimination with grace (Galatians 3:28).
- Building Bridges: Engaging in dialogue and empathy across differences.
- Conclusion: Challenging listeners to pursue unity and reconciliation through the practice of grace.

Chapter 5

Message: God's heart for the lost One

Scripture: Ezekiel 34:16

The parable of the lost sheep illustrates God's heart for seeking the lost and bringing them back into His Kingdom.

This passage shows the deep compassion of God towards those who have strayed, emphasizing His relentless pursuit of each individual who wanders away from His fold. Just as a shepherd leaves the ninety-nine sheep to find the one that is lost.

Throughout the Bible, we see numerous examples of God's initiative in seeking the lost. In Ezekiel 34:16, the Lord promises, "I will seek the lost, and I will bring back the strayed, and I will bind up the injured, and I will strengthen the weak."

These declarations assured us of God's commitment to actively searching for those who have indeed gone astray, demonstrating His unwavering love and desire for their return.

Further on, Jesus describes Himself as the Good Shepherd who willingly lays down His life for His sheep (John 10:11). His sacrificial love extends beyond mere words; it is an active action that exemplifies His determination to rescue humanity from sin and spiritual darkness. As followers, we are to embody this same spirit to seek the lost for the Kingdom.

It is commanded in Matthew 28:19-20 "go therefore and make disciples of all nations, baptizing them in the name of the Father, of the Son and of the Holy Spirit, teaching them to observe all that I have commanded you."

We are, therefore, called to spread God's work of reconciliation, bringing the message of hope and salvation to a world in need of His everlasting love.

Just as the earthly shepherd rejoices over finding the lost sheep, heaven celebrates if and when one sinner repents (Luke 15:7), affirming the immeasurable value God places on each individual and His boundless joy in their return to Him.

Chapter 6

Message: Whoever has an ear let them hear

Scripture: Revelations 2:2-7

The words of the Lord resonate clearly in Revelations 2:2-7: "He who has an ear, let him hear what the Spirit says to the churches." These words become a sounding board through time, calling upon us to listen not just with our ears, but with the depths of our hearts and souls. Let us cultivate ears that are attuned to His Spirit, receptive to His teachings, and responsive in obedience.

The Lord commended the church in Ephesus for their perseverance and discernment against false teachings, yet they were chastised for losing their first love. This serves as a stark reminder that while doctrinal purity is crucial, it is equally vital to maintain a fervent love for God and for one another.

John 15:4-5 further clarifies this truth: "Abide in me, and I in you. As the branch cannot bear fruit by itself, unless it abides in the vine, neither can you, unless you abide in me. I am the vine; you are the branches."

“Whoever abides in me and I in him, it is he that will bear much fruit, for apart from me you can do nothing." Here, Jesus emphasizes the intimate connection we must have with Him—like branches to a vine—that bear fruit that glorifies God. This abiding requires active listening, a continuous tuning of our hearts to His voice amidst the noise of the world.

We are called not merely to hear, but to heed. To hear with intentionality and depth, understanding that the Word of God is alive and active (Hebrews 4:12). It penetrates to the division of soul and of spirit, of joints and of marrow, discerning the thoughts and intentions of the heart.

As we do so, we position ourselves to receive the fullness of His promises and to walk in the paths of righteousness.

In a world filled with distractions and competing voices, may we be like the church in Philadelphia, whom Jesus praised for their faithful endurance and obedience. Let us hold fast to what we have, keeping His word and not denying His name.

Chapter 7
Message: The unmovable commitment

Scripture: 1 Corinthians 15:58

The Apostle Paul's directive in 1 Corinthians 15:58 serves as a reminder that every act of service, no matter how small, contributes to a greater divine purpose. Church members are encouraged to view their work through an eternal perspective, where their labor in the Lord is seen as part of a grander scheme that transcends temporal concerns.

This perspective should not only motivate individuals to give their best but also help them to find joy and fulfillment in their roles.

Personally, I can testify to the faithfulness of a number of individuals who fit this description in our congregation here at First Baptist Church of Randolph, Massachusetts.

The assurance that their labor is not in vain imbues their service with a sense of dignity and hope, fueling an ongoing commitment to the work of the Lord with unwavering enthusiasm.

The apostle's description again of being "immovable" also suggests a commitment to unity and purpose within the church community.

Members are urged to support one another, fostering an environment where collective efforts are directed towards common goals. This also is very evident in our local congregation.

This unity is critical, as it amplifies our effectiveness, and ensures that our combined efforts are not thwarted by internal discord or external pressures usually instigated by the enemy.

The strength and growth of the Kingdom Church as a whole depends on each member's individual commitment to remain anchored in our shared mission, thereby creating a resilient and harmonious body of believers who are fully committed to this shared goal of serving the Kingdom of God.

Chapter 8

Message: Your giants are no match for the Lord

Scripture: 1 Samuel 17

One of my favorite books in the bible, Samuel, tells a powerful story of a biblical account of young David and warrior Goliath, the soldier. In this account, the Philistine giant Goliath, challenges the nation of Israelites to send out a champion to fight him in a single combat, asserting that the outcome of this fight will determine the fate of both armies.

Here comes the rest of the story of the next King of Israel. Goliath, described as a colossal warrior clad in heavy armor and armed with formidable weapons, taunts the Israelites and defies their God. His challenge strikes fear into the heart of King Saul and the Israelite soldiers, who are intimidated by Goliath's imposing presence and his record of victories.

In this backdrop of despair and fear, young David, a shepherd boy and the youngest of eight brothers, enters the scene. David has been sent by his father, Jesse, to deliver provisions to his older brothers who are serving in Saul's army. Upon hearing Goliath's defiant challenge, David expresses his willingness to fight the giant, despite his youth and lack of military experience.

His confidence stems from his faith in God and his previous experiences defending his flock from lions and bears. David's boldness is initially met with skepticism and mockery, but he persists, arguing that the Lord who delivered him from the claws of predators will deliver him from Goliath.

The confrontation unfolds with dramatic intensity. David, using his sling and a single stone, strikes Goliath on the forehead, causing the giant to fall to the ground. David then uses Goliath's own sword to behead him, securing a decisive victory for the Israelites.

This event not only demonstrates David's bravery and faith but also serves as the ultimate symbol of divine intervention and the triumph of righteousness over overwhelming odds.

The victory over Goliath leads to a significant shift in the narrative, setting the stage for David's future as a key figure in Israel's history, and underscoring the definitive fact that faith in God can lead to extraordinary triumphs against seemingly insurmountable challenges.

Chapter 9
Message: How gifted we are

Scripture: 1 Corinthians 12: 4-11

Apostle Paul's letter to the Corinth church acknowledges that, the Corinthian believers have been enriched in various ways, particularly in their speech and knowledge, which reflect the grace of God.

Paul's statement also suggests that the church has been endowed with various spiritual gifts, enabling them to excel in their understanding and communication of the faith.

This introduction sets the tone for the letter, highlighting both the blessings and the potential for growth within the community.

Paul's gratitude is not just a general expression of thanks but a recognition of the specific ways in which God's grace has been manifested in the lives of the Corinthian believers.

The mention of their enrichment in speech and knowledge underscores the transforming power of divine grace, which equips them to articulate and comprehend the gospel message.

This acceptance also serves as a prelude to addressing the issues of division and discord within the church, illustrating that while the Corinthians have been richly blessed, there are still areas that need attention and correction.

The passage also contains a forward-looking perspective, as Paul alludes to the anticipation of Christ's return. He reassures the Corinthians that their current state of spiritual enrichment is a preparation for the ultimate revelation of Jesus Christ.

This eschatological dimension reinforces the idea that their present gifts and knowledge are not ends in themselves but are meant to prepare them for future fulfillment.

The expectation of Christ's return provides a context for understanding their current experiences and challenges within the faith community.

Finally, Paul mentions that he has been informed of quarrels among them, indicating that despite their spiritual gifts, the church is struggling with internal strife.

Look around you, do you see and hear what the apostle heard of the Corinth Church? If we don't live in His grace, our gifts will become a hindrance, not a blessing, as it is intended.

Chapter 10

Message: The power of God in the Gospels

Scripture: 1 Corinthians 2:4-5

1 Corinthians 2:4-5, Paul brings us to the role of divine wisdom and power in the message of the Gospel. He gives a powerful exhortation, "My speech and my preaching were not with persuasive words of human wisdom, but in demonstration of the Spirit and of power." This passage highlights the contrast between human eloquence and the changing impact of the Holy Spirit.

Paul seeks to remind the Corinthian believers that the essence of his message is rooted not in rhetorical skill but in the work of God, which invites a deeper understanding of faith beyond mere intellectual assent. Paul's approach to preaching reflects a deliberate choice to prioritize the Spirit's power over worldly wisdom.

In a culture that values persuasive speech and philosophical reasoning, Paul's commitment to a Gospel rooted in spiritual authority challenges conventional expectations. He understands that genuine conviction and faith arise from the heart, not from well-crafted arguments.

By relying on the Holy Spirit, Paul underscores the fact that, it is God's power that ultimately brings about change and transforms lives, rather than mortal human effort or persuasion. Furthermore, Paul stresses the importance of faith being grounded in God's power rather than human wisdom. He states, "That your faith should not be in the wisdom of men but in the power of God."

This assertion serves as a reminder that the foundation of the Christian faith is not based on human understanding or intellectual achievement but on the divine revelation of God through Jesus Christ. This distinction invites believers to seek a deeper relationship with God, one that is anchored in trust and reliance on His sovereignty.

In conclusion, this Scripture challenges believers to reflect on the source of their faith and the nature of their witness, by focusing on the Spirit's power rather than mortal human wisdom.

Paul calls us to experience the transforming work of God in our lives and encourages us to embrace a faith that goes beyond intellectual understanding, fostering a deeper reliance on God's ability to work within and through us.

Chapter 11

Message: The Awakening Hope

(The pre-advent message)

Scripture: Isaiah 40:31

As we approach the season of Advent, a time of preparation and anticipation, we are called to awaken to hope. In Isaiah 40:31, we find a promise: "But those who hope in the Lord will renew their strength.

They will soar on wings like eagles; they will run and not grow weary; they will walk and not be faint." A reminder that hope is not merely a fleeting sentiment, but a life-giving force rooted in our faith in God.

In a world that often feels heavy with uncertainty and despair, we are invited to look beyond our circumstances and place our trust in the One who sustains us.

The imagery of soaring like eagles speaks to the transformative power of hope. Eagles are known for their ability to rise high above the storms, utilizing the winds to lift them to greater heights.

Similarly, when we cultivate hope in our hearts, we can rise above the challenges we face. Advent is a time to reflect on the ways in which our hope can be renewed.

As we prepare to celebrate the coming of Christ, we are reminded that He embodies the hope we seek—a hope that transcends our trials and invites us into a deeper relationship with God.

In practical terms, awakening to hope requires us to shift our focus from the obstacles in our path to the promises of God. It calls us to engage in spiritual practices that nurture our souls—prayer, scripture reading, and acts of service.

Each of these practices can help us ground ourselves in the truth that God is with us, guiding and strengthening us. By doing so, we align ourselves with the assurance found in Isaiah that those who hope in the Lord will not only endure but will thrive, finding renewed strength for the journey ahead.

In this period of pre-Advent journey, let us commit to awakening to the hope that is ours in Christ. May we be inspired to rise above our weariness and doubts, embracing the promise that God is our source of strength.

Let us enter this season with open hearts, ready to receive the hope that comes from waiting expectantly for the celebration of Christ's birth. In this act of waiting, may we discover the depth of God's love and the power of hope, allowing it to lift us into a season of renewal and joy.

Chapter 12

Message: The Faithful in Preparation

(A Pre-advent message)

Scripture: Matthew 25:1-13

In the parable of the ten virgins, as found in the book of Matthew 25:1-13, Jesus speaks to the importance of preparation, as we wait for the unexpected arrival of the bridegroom. The story depicts ten virgins who took their lamps and went out to meet the bridegroom. Five of them were wise, bringing extra oil for their lamps, while the other five were foolish and brought none.

When the bridegroom was delayed, all ten fell asleep. However, when the announcement was made about his arrival, only the wise virgins were ready, highlighting the critical nature of preparedness in faith.

The wise virgins represent those who are diligent in their spiritual preparation. Their foresight in bringing additional oil symbolizes the need for an ongoing relationship with God, marked by prayer, study of Scripture, and acts of service.

This proactive approach to faith ensures that they can endure the waiting period and respond promptly when opportunities for service and worship arise. In contrast, the foolish virgin's lack of preparation reflects a complacent attitude towards their faith.

When the moment of truth arrived, they were unprepared for the occasion, demonstrating the consequences of neglecting spiritual responsibilities. Jesus's teaching in this parable serves as a reminder that faith is not merely about belief but also about action and readiness.

The urgency of the bridegroom's surprise arrival signifies the unexpected nature of Christ's return and the need for vigilance in our spiritual lives. Believers are called to be watchful and to cultivate their faith continually, ensuring they have enough "oil" to sustain their daily living during times of waiting and uncertainty. This preparation requires intentionality, as it is easy to become distracted and complacent, especially in a world filled with competing priorities.

Ultimately, the parable concludes with a sobering truth: the door was shut for the foolish virgins when they returned, stressing the finality of their unpreparedness.

"Faithful in preparation" encourages believers to actively engage in their faith, ensuring they are not only waiting for Christ's return but are also living out their faith in tangible ways.

Chapter 13
Message: The Gift of Gratitude

Scripture: 1 Thessalonians 5:16-18

Apostle Paul offers a succinct yet wonderful message about the importance of gratitude in a believer. He encourages the Thessalonians to "rejoice always," to "pray continually," and to "give thanks in all circumstances."

This tri-part exhortation emphasizes that gratitude is not just a response to favorable situations, but it should be a continuous attitude of the heart of the believer.

The call to give thanks "in all circumstances" underscores the power of gratitude in shaping our perspectives and experiences. Gratitude, as presented in this passage, is a gift that cultivates joy and peace.

When we adopt a posture of thankfulness, we shift our focus from what we lack to the abundance we possess. This shift can be particularly powerful in challenging times, where it is easy to dwell on difficulties and disappointments.

By choosing to acknowledge and appreciate the blessings in our lives, even amid trials, we can experience a deeper sense of contentment. The act of gratitude fosters resilience, enabling us to navigate life's ups and downs with a more positive outlook.

Ultimately, the gift serves as a vital expression of faith. Paul emphasizes that giving thanks is "God's will for you in Christ Jesus," reminding us that gratitude aligns us with God's purposes.

When we embrace it, we embody a lifestyle that reflects our trust in God's goodness and sovereignty.

This attitude not only enriches our personal faith journey but also serves as a witness to others, we invite others to experience the joy and peace that come from recognizing and celebrating the blessings of God, thereby creating a ripple effect of thankfulness in our communities.

Indeed, in this time of expectation of the second coming of our Lord and Savior, we should all be gracious to God and to one another, Amen.

Chapter 14
Message: Light in the darkness

Scripture: John 1:4-5

In John 1:4-5 (NIV), we read, "In him was life, and that life was the light of all mankind. The light shines in the darkness, and the darkness has not overcome it."

This passage introduces us to the essential nature of Christ as both life and light. The Light of Christ Jesus brings us hope and truth, while darkness brings us into despair, confusion, and sin, ultimately sending us into eternal damnation.

The imagery is powerful: Jesus is the light that breaks into our darkened world, illuminating our path and offering a way out of the shadows of despair. To understand the meaning of this light begins with recognizing the darkness we face in our lives.

Darkness can manifest in various forms—spiritual emptiness, emotional struggles, or moral dilemmas. Many people wander through life feeling lost or trapped, searching for meaning and purpose.

In these moments, the light of Christ becomes not just a beacon of hope but an invitation to a transformed life. He purposefully enters our darkness, shining brightly, and challenges us to confront our fears, doubts, and sins.

Moreover, the light of Christ empowers us to shine in the world around us. As believers, we are called to reflect His light in our communities, spreading hope and truth to those still in darkness.

This calling is not merely an obligation; it is a privilege. By embodying Christ's love and compassion, we can brighten the lives of others, offering support and guidance to those struggling to find their way. Our light can lead others to the true source in life and transformation, inviting them to experience the same hope that has changed us, Jesus Christ, Amen.

Ultimately, we know that "the darkness has not overcome it," reminding us of the victory we have in Christ. No matter how overwhelming the darkness may seem, it cannot extinguish the light of Jesus. This promise gives us the courage to face our own darkness and to share that light with others.

In a world filled with uncertainty, let us embrace our role as bearers of light, shining brightly amidst the shadows, and proclaiming the truth that in Christ, hope and life are always within reach, Amen.

Chapter 15

Message: Receiving all that God has spoken concerning us

Scripture: Isaiah 58:14

Good evening, saints. Thank you, Pastor Ron and first lady, for your invitation, but most importantly, for your leadership in this community.

By the way, both spiritually and socially, it is indeed a blessing that the late Cheryl Frazier and I spoke about all the time.

Today, we turn our hearts to the powerful truth found in Prophet Isaiah book, chapter 58:14:

"Then you will find your joy in the Lord, and I will cause you to ride on the heights of the land and to feast on the inheritance of your father Jacob."

This promise is a beautiful invitation to "receive all that God has spoken concerning us," someone say Amen!

However, to realize its full weight, we need to understand the context of the full chapter of Isaiah 58 and explore its relevance for us in today's church.

Context of Isaiah 58:

Isaiah 58 addresses the people of Israel at a time when their religious practices had become mere rituals devoid of genuine meaning. Does it feel familiar to you as you look around churches near and far today?

The chapter begins with God calling out their empty fasting—though they appeared to seek Him, their actions revealed a disconnect between their worship and their daily lives.

They exploited their workers, had hateful disagreements, and failed to care for the needy, few of the charges levied against them, as a people.

The Lord uses Isaiah to challenge them, revealing that true fasting is about social justice and compassion, not just outward shows of piety and symbolism.

A message I recently heard, spoken by one Rev. Augustus Corbett, reminds me that Psalm 89:14 speaks about two things; "Righteousness and justice are the foundation of your throne, love and faithfulness go before you".

This passage tells us that God's throne is established on these two principles, so how come some churches love to quote you only the righteousness piece, but not the Justice part.

Again, Isaiah 1:17 also tells us to "Learn to do right; seek justice. Defend the oppressed. Take up the cause of the fatherless; plead the case of the widows".

Isaiah once again reminds us that "The Spirit of the Lord is upon me to preach the gospel to the poor."

All these chapters I just quoted call us back to the essence of what it means to honor God through our actions, both spiritually and socially.

So, please indulge me a little time tonight as we navigate through this tri-part message of Chapter 58:14, and a few conclusional comments. Can I get your permission, church? If Ok, say Amen! So, say the people, Pastor Ron.

The Joy of the Lord:

In Isaiah 58:14, we see a transforming promise: "Then you will find your joy in the Lord."

This joy is profound, not contingent on external circumstances but rooted in our relationship with God.

Nehemiah 8:10 reminds us, "The joy of the Lord is your strength." When we align our hearts with God's purposes—caring for the marginalized and serving others—we tap into a deep well of joy that sustains us.

You see friends, in a world where many chase temporary happiness, the church must model this enduring joy that comes from fulfilling God's commandments.

Riding on the Heights:

The second part of Isaiah 58:14 promises, "I will cause you to ride on the heights of the land." Riding on the heights symbolizes spiritual elevation and divine favor, now, this is when you Amen!

Tell the story of eagles swooping through the fields with powerful, majestic wings.

Isaiah 40:31; But those who hope in the Lord will renew their strength. They will soar on wings like eagles; they will run and not grow weary; they will walk and not be faint.

This imagery suggests that when we commit to living out God's call to justice and mercy, He elevates us above our struggles.

In Romans 8:37, Paul declares, "No, in all these things we are more than conquerors through him who loved us." He continues by saying....

38, For I am convinced that neither death nor life, neither angels nor demons, neither the present nor the future nor any powers,

39, neither heights nor depths, nor anything else in all creation will be able to separate us from the love of God....wait for it that is in Christ Jesus our Lord, now you can say Amen.

So, let me ask you again? Why do we worry? If we are in Him, and are caring for His people, the poor, the homeless, the dejected, those incarcerated, and the unsaved, then nothing can separate us from His eternal Love.

This message should resonate deeply in our church setting today, where many face challenges and despair.

God invites us to rise above these difficulties through faithful obedience and trust in His promises.

Feasting on the Inheritance:

The final part of our verse, "to feast on the inheritance of your father Jacob," speaks of God's abundant provision.

Brethren, our inheritance as children of God includes not only spiritual blessings but also a calling to reflect His character in the world.

Ephesians 1:18 reminds us of the riches of His glorious inheritance in the saints.

Today's church often forgets this truth; we are heirs of a promise that empowers us to live abundantly and share that abundance with others.

We must reclaim our identity as God's beloved children, embracing the fullness of life He offers.

Call to Genuine Worship:

As we reflect on these truths, we must examine our worship practices. Are we engaging in genuine worship, or are we simply fulfilling religious obligations?

God desires our hearts, not just our rituals. In John 4:24, Jesus tells us, "God is spirit, and his worshipers must worship Him in the Spirit and in truth."

True worship manifests in how we treat others and how we live our daily lives. To most, the closest they experience the goodness of God, is through a kind word, a smile, a hello, or simply a presence of listening.

Today, the church must be known not just for our gatherings but for our commitment to justice, mercy, and love through our various ministries.

Be proactive in the reception of God's promises:

"Receiving all that God has spoken concerning us" requires a proactive response.

As Isaiah challenges the Israelites to move beyond empty rituals, we too, must seek a deeper relationship with God.

This journey involves prayer, studying His Word, and actively serving those in need.

Philippians 4:19 assures us, “And my God will meet all your needs according to the riches of his glory in Christ Jesus.”

Friends, when we align our lives with God’s heart, we open ourselves to receive the fullness of His promises.

Conclusion:

In conclusion, Isaiah 58:14 is a clear and urgent call for us to receive all that God has spoken concerning us.

We must remember the weight of God’s declaration: “The mouth of the Lord has spoken.”

We are reminded of the authority and certainty of God’s promise. You see friends, it is not a suggestion but a commitment from God to His people, You and I, Amen.

As we strive to align ourselves with God’s will, let us hold fast to His promises.

As we find our joy in Him, ride on the heights, and feast on our inheritance, let us commit to being a church that reflects His love and justice.

I don’t know about you, but with me, I find out that in my obedience and service to Him, I always find my joy, and experience elevation in my spiritual life, even as I partake in this rich inheritance offered to me.

Will you also try it today? Join me in this wonderful, amazing connection, and deeper relationship with our Father, through His Son, Jesus the Christ.

May we be a community that embodies these principles, transforming our world by sharing the joy and hope we find in Christ.

So, Spring of water fellowship, Let us respond to God's invitation with open hearts, ready to embrace the abundant life He offers. Amen.

Let us Pray:

Heavenly Father,

We thank You for Your Word, and the awesome truth found in Isaiah 58:14.

Help us to be a Church that seeks Your heart, a community that embodies Your love, and a people who actively pursue justice and mercy.

May we find our joy in You and live out our calling as Your heirs. In Jesus's mighty name, we pray,

Amen.

Chapter 16

Message: The Triumphal Entry

Welcoming the King into Our Hearts

Scripture: Matthew 21: 1-11

Friends, this story of Jesus's triumphal entry into Jerusalem was unfolding with a sense of anticipation and symbolism.

We are told that, as Jesus approaches Jerusalem, He instructs His disciples to procure a donkey and its colt, fulfilling a prophecy from Zechariah, but we will get to the prophecy soon.

This deliberate act underscores the significance of Jesus's arrival and the fulfillment of these ancient prophecies regarding the Messiah.

The atmosphere is charged with excitement as crowds gather, laying their cloaks and palm branches on the road, symbolizing a gesture of honor and recognition of Jesus as the long-awaited King of Israel.

The scene becomes even more celebratory as Jesus rides into Jerusalem on the donkey, echoing the image of a humble yet triumphant king.

The people's response is one of jubilation, shouting "Hosanna to the

Son of David!" and acknowledging Jesus as the one who comes in the name of the Lord.

This momentous occasion marks a pivotal point in Jesus's ministry, as he publicly declares His identity and purpose, despite knowing the events that will soon unfold.

The symbolism of the donkey, a humble beast of burden, contrasts sharply with the image of a conquering king riding on a warhorse, explain!

This deliberate choice reinforces Jesus's message of humility and peace, challenging the conventional notions of power and authority.

So, this entry has set the stage for the dramatic events that will follow, leading ultimately to Jesus's crucifixion and resurrection, thereby fulfilling the divine plan for redemption.

What was the purpose of all these theatricals, where is it's Scriptural Foundation?

Matthew 21:1-11.

As they approached Jerusalem and came to Bethphage on the Mount of Olives, Jesus sent two disciples,

> 2 saying to them, "Go to the village ahead of you, and at once you will find a donkey tied there, with her colt by her. Untie them and bring them to me.
>
> 3 If anyone says anything to you, say that the Lord needs them, and he will send them right away."
>
> 4 This took place to fulfill what was spoken through the prophet:
>
> 5 "Say to Daughter Zion,

'See, your king comes to you,

gentle and riding on a donkey,

and on a colt, the foal of a donkey.'

6 The disciples went and did as Jesus had instructed them.

7 They brought the donkey and the colt and placed their cloaks on them for Jesus to sit on.

8 A very large crowd spread their cloaks on the road, while others cut branches from the trees and spread them on the road.

9 The crowds that went ahead of him and those that followed shouted,

"Hosanna to the Son of David!"

"Blessed is he who comes in the name of the Lord!"

"Hosanna in the highest heaven!"

10 When Jesus entered Jerusalem, the whole city was stirred and asked, "Who is this?"

11 The crowds answered, "This is Jesus, the prophet from Nazareth in Galilee."

Please take these five (5) points notes for your study....

1. Fulfillment of Prophecy:

The prophet Zechariah foretold the coming of the Messiah, proclaiming, "Rejoice greatly, O daughter of Zion! Shout, Daughter of Jerusalem! See, your king comes to you, righteous and victorious, lowly, and riding on a donkey, on a colt, the foal of a donkey" (Zechariah 9:9). This prophecy finds its fulfillment in Jesus' entry into Jerusalem.

2. The King's Humility & it's symbolism:

Jesus's choice to enter Jerusalem on a donkey rather than a horse carries great symbolism.

In a culture where triumphal entries were often accompanied by displays of military might and grandeur, for example; King David returning from one of his various victorious wars.

Jesus's humble mode of transportation demonstrates His rejection of worldly pomp and His embrace of humility.

This act underscores His message of servant leadership and His mission to establish a kingdom rooted in love and compassion, why don't you and I take a clue from Jesus.

Jesus, the King of kings, chose to enter Jerusalem not on a majestic horse, but on a humble donkey, yet today you have Pastors who want a bigger story than the one given to them to preach. Someone say Amen!

Again, let me repeat...this act symbolized His humility and peaceful intentions. Despite being the Messiah, Jesus did not seek earthly grandeur or power but embodied humility and servanthood.

3. The Response of the People:

As Jesus entered Jerusalem, the crowds hailed Him as the Son of David, acknowledging His royal lineage and Messianic identity.

They laid palm branches and cloaks before Him, with shouts of "Hosanna!" which means "Save, we pray!" They recognized Jesus as their long-awaited Messiah, the One who would bring salvation to God's people.

Their enthusiastic response reflects their hope and expectation for deliverance. Signifying their recognition of His authority and their hope for deliverance (Matthew 21:8-9).

This moment serves as a powerful declaration of Jesus' kingship and His role as the Savior of God's people.

4. The Contrast of Expectations:

While the crowds hailed Jesus as the Son of David, acknowledging His royal lineage, the religious leaders of the time viewed Him with suspicion and disdain. But also, how many of us have thought about this contrast...

"The symbolism of the donkey, a humble beast of burden, contrasts sharply with the image of a conquering king riding on a warhorse."

As we know later, This deliberate choice reinforces Jesus's message of humility and peace, challenging the conventional notions of power and authority.

Verses [23] Jesus entered the temple courts, and, while he was teaching, the chief priests and the elders of the people came to him. "By what authority are you doing these things?" they asked. "And who gave you this authority?"

[24] Jesus replied, "I will also ask you one question. If you answer me, I will tell you by what authority I am doing these things. [25] John's baptism—where did it come from? Was it from heaven, or of human origin?"

They discussed it among themselves and said, "If we say, 'From heaven,' he will ask, 'Then why didn't you believe him?' [26] But if we say, 'Of human origin'—we are afraid of the people, for they all hold that John was a prophet."

[27] So they answered Jesus, "We don't know. "Then He said, "Neither will I tell you by what authority I am doing these things.

They were threatened by His popularity and feared losing their authority. This contrast highlights the spiritual blindness of those who failed to recognize Jesus as the promised Messiah.

5. The Invitation to Personal Transformation:

Jesus entered Jerusalem amidst shouts of praise and adoration, He desires to enter into our hearts today. We are likewise invited to respond to His presence in our lives.

His triumphal entry symbolizes the invitation for each of us to welcome Him as our King and Savior.

As we journey through Holy Week, let us prepare our hearts to receive Jesus anew and allow Him to reign over every aspect of our lives.

Brothers and sisters, This entry also serves as a reminder of the ongoing invitation for each of us to recognize Jesus as our King and Savior, to lay down our lives before Him in submission and worship, and to participate in His kingdom mission of love, justice, and reconciliation.

In Conclusion:

The triumphal entry of Jesus into Jerusalem serves as a reminder of His kingship, humility, and ultimate mission of redemption.

Let us walk with Him through this Holy Week, embracing His sacrifice on the cross and celebrating His glorious resurrection.

May His kingdom come, and His will be done, on earth as it is in heaven. Amen.

Chapter 17
Message: Is God Listening?

Scripture Reading: Habakkuk 1:1-4; 2:1-4

Good morning, beloved congregation. Today, I would like to ask you a question? "Is God listening?"

This question came into mind as I was one morning doing a quiet time in the book of Habakkuk, You see friends, a prophetic dialogue was taking place between the prophet and God, can you imagine this exchange?

The last time such a conversation took place was between, Moses and "I am" and also between Job and "Yahweh" on his suffering, which, by the way, was precepted by again a conversation between God and "Lucifer", you get the picture?

According to Scripture, these conversations don't end well for the created beings, God always wins the arguments, and this one by the Prophet Habakkuk was no different.

Even though Habakkuk's context of this particular account in Scripture is ancient, his questions and the answers that he received from God still resonate deeply with our own world today.

Especially because of all the political upheavals, injustices, bold-faced lies, and Using God's name to achieve our end goals. Yes, as I remind you, Habakkuk as a prophet who lived in a time of this great injustice, corruption, and uncertainty. Indeed, there is not much of a different today. Look around, listen to TV, political pundits, and podcasts.

As our good intention, global leaders struggle to address climate change, economic inequality, and geopolitical tensions.

It can often feel as though God is silent or distant, leaving us questioning whether divine justice is truly at work.

God's response to Habakkuk offers both challenge and hope. He reveals that He is indeed at work, though His methods may seem different than ours.

God's plan involves raising up the Babylonians as agents of judgment, a revelation that underscores the complexity of divine intervention.

For us, this means recognizing that God's ways may not align with our expectations or timelines.

The upheavals and crises we witness could be part of a larger divine narrative that we might not fully understand, yet which is ultimately underpinned by God's justice and sovereignty.

His experience and the responses he received from God offer us an insight into our own struggles and questions about divine silence in our world today, some might say, where is God?

Is He listening to our cry for judgment against the unjust, and the rebellious attitudes of modern society?

First, let us dig a little deeper into what the Prophet was lamenting about.

I. The lamentation of the Prophet- (Habakkuk 1:1-4)

Habakkuk opens his book with a cry of desperation: “How long, Lord, must I call for help, but you do not listen?

Or cry out to you, ‘Violence!’ but you do not save? Why do you make me look at injustice? Why do you tolerate wrongdoing?”

It sounds like he is more concerned about how God is making him look like a prophet rather than being the instrument he is...you see, my dear friends, instruments are supposed to bend to which ever direction the author pleases, hello somebody?

Are you more interested in how serving God makes you look? Rather than being the obedient clay that can be molded into whichever direction He pleases?

Don’t get me wrong, sometimes our actions are like Habakkuk’s questions, Yes, raw and genuine.

Yet we do not have the right to question God, He responded to Job’s question with a question; where were you when I created the earth?

You see friends, from where Habakkuk stands, like you and me, in today’s political atmosphere, he sees violence and injustice all around him and wonders why God seems distant.

His lament is not just for his time but for every age when the human experience is marred by suffering and injustice.

You and I today: We, too, live in a world rife with injustice and turmoil. Wars, systemic corruption, economic disparities, and a climate crisis that threatens our very existence—these issues can make us feel as though God is silent.

In our personal lives, we face trials that may seem overwhelming, and it's easy to question whether God is truly listening. (Give the Haitian experience in the park)

The answer = Yes, He knows your question before you ask...so, yes, He is listening, but it does not mean we will always like the answer. So, what was God's answer?

II. God's Response (Habakkuk 1:5-11)

God's response to Habakkuk's crying is surprising. He tells Habakkuk to look and be amazed because He is raising up the Babylonians, a fierce and ruthless nation, to bring judgment.

Could it be true today that because of our rebellious attitude, God has raised a "Babylonians" to bring judgment on us even now?

"Look at the nations and watch—and be utterly amazed. For I am going to do something in your days that you would not believe, even if you were told."

God's answer is startling. He does not provide the reassurance Habakkuk might have expected. Instead,

He reveals that He is at work in ways that are beyond human understanding. This response underscores that God's ways are higher than our ways, and His plans are not always immediately clear or comfortable.

You and I today: In our context, God's ways may also seem perplexing. We may not see immediate solutions to global crises or personal challenges.

However, this passage reminds us that God is sovereign and active, even when His methods are beyond our comprehension. His justice and mercy are working in ways we might not see or understand.

III. The Call to Faith (Habakkuk 2:1-4)

Habakkuk's dialogue with God leads him to a place of watchfulness and faith: "I will stand at my watch and station myself on the ramparts; I will look to see what He will say to me, and what answer I am to give to this complaint.

Then the Lord replied: 'Write down the revelation and make it plain on tablets so that a herald may run with it.

For the revelation awaits an appointed time; it speaks of the end and will not prove false. Though it lingers, wait for it.

It will certainly come and will not delay. "See, the enemy is puffed up; his desires are not upright—but the righteous person will live by his faithfulness."

God calls Habakkuk to a posture of vigilance and patience. The promise is that God's plan will unfold in its appointed time, and the righteous will live by faith.

This is a sacred call to trust in God's timing and sovereignty, even when the world seems to be in chaos.

You and I today: For us, this passage calls us to adopt a similar posture. In a world filled with uncertainty, we are invited to live by faith.

The righteous will live by their faithfulness, trusting that God's plan is unfolding, even when it is not immediately apparent. Our faith is not based on what we see, but on the character and promises of God.

The conclusion and So what?

As we bring this message to an end, remember, In the midst of our struggles, Habakkuk's story reminds us that God is indeed listening, even when it seems like He is silent.

God's ways are mysterious, His timing is perfect, and His plans are good. We are called to live by faith, standing firm on the promises of God and trusting that His justice will ultimately prevail.

As we face the challenges of our time, let us remember that God is not distant but is actively working in ways that we might not fully understand.

Habakkuk's story encourages us to adopt a stance of patient faith. Despite the seeming delay of justice, God assures that His plan will unfold in its own time, and "the righteous person will live by his faithfulness."

In our turbulent world, this call to faithfulness invites us to trust that God is listening and working behind the scenes.

It also challenges us to remain steadfast and hopeful, to act justly and compassionately, and to support efforts that align with God's vision for peace and righteousness.

Our call is to remain vigilant, hopeful, and faithful, knowing that in the end, God's kingdom will come, and His will be done.

Let us continue to pray for the strength to live by faith, the wisdom to see God's hand in our world, and the courage to act justly and love mercy as we walk humbly with our God.

Amen.

Chapter 18

Message: The planted seed in our youth, harvested in our adulthood

Scripture Reading: 1 Chronicles 21:16-30

1 Chronicles 21:16-30 has become one of my go-to biblical guides into God's pronouncement on biblical views and principles on seed planting in our early years and its effects later years.

You see, friends, the golden light of the setting sun cast long shadows over the city of Jerusalem. On a quiet hill, not far from the bustling streets.

Here, King David of now known Israel, stood still, his gazed eyes fixed upon the threshing floor of Ornan, a place now well-known for its spiritual significance. His heart was heavy, knowing the weight of his planted seeds and recent actions and their consequences.

The angel's message was clear: according to first Chronicles, "build an altar to the Lord on the threshing floor of Ornan". It was here that David's faith and resolve would be tested.

This place, where grains were once separated from chaff, would now become a sacred site where David would seek God's favor and offer a sacrifice of repentance.

This Scripture presents us with a vivid portrayal of David's response to a pivotal moment in his life, where we see the principles of sowing and reaping unfold before us.

The passage not only highlights the consequences of our actions but also teaches us about the seeds we plant in our youth and the harvest we can expect in our adulthood.

The context of the passage:

In our reading, King David is instructed by the angel of the Lord to build an altar to the Lord on the threshing floor of Ornan (or Arunah).

The angel of the Lord's appearance to David, this majestic being with a sword, was not there to chit-chat. He was bringing a message of judgment upon Israel.

David, overwhelmed by the sight of this majestic angel, and the devastation it had proclaimed, fell to his knees and prayed earnestly, pleading for mercy.

His heart ached with the realization that his own decisions had led to this sorrow. When David approached Ornan, who was on his threshing floor, working with his oxen.

Ornan looked up, surprised to see the king himself. The sight of David, accompanied by his men, was unusual for such a humble location.

This threshing floor, located on Mount Moriah, becomes a significant place of worship and sacrifice.

David's willingness to purchase the site and build an altar on it demonstrates his commitment to God, even in the face of hardship and personal cost.

The cost of the seed of disobedience:

Pastor, what are you talking about? Going back to verses 1-16 in 1 Chronicles; we're told that King David's disobedience to God is shown through his decision to conduct a census of Israel. Driven by a sense of pride and a desire to gauge the extent of his military strength.

David orders a count of the fighting men in his kingdom, despite being advised against it by Joab, his commander.

This act is perceived as a lack of trust in God's ability to sustain and protect Israel. Have you ever said, this is not enough, even when the Lord says it is?

You see, this action is indicating a shift from reliance on divine guidance to human metrics of power and control. Do you see that in our churches and government?

The story suggests this action was not merely a bureaucratic decision but a deeper moral and spiritual lapse, as David's choice to number the people reveals a troubling inclination towards self-reliance and pride.

As we will see, God's response to David's disobedience is swift and severe. As a consequence of the census, a divine punishment is enacted, and Israel is struck with a plague that results in the death of seventy thousand people.

This catastrophic outcome underscores the gravity of David's error, But praise God, that is not the end of the story.

David's subsequent repentance and his plea for God's mercy will highlight his recognition of the magnitude of his transgression.

However, the devastating impact of his actions on the nation serves as a reminder of the consequences of deviating from divine commands in each and every one of our lives. Our youthful indiscretions follow us into adulthood.

Now, the good news! The Seed of Obedience:

"Why have you come, my king?" continuing the story-Ornan asked, setting aside his tools and bowing respectfully.

David stepped forward with a heavy heart. “I have come to buy your threshing floor,” he said earnestly. “I need to build an altar to the Lord here, to offer sacrifices and seek His mercy.”

But you’re the King, you could have sent someone! (Paraphrasing)

Ornan’s eyes widened in astonishment. “Let my lord the king take whatever he needs,” Ornan said, his voice filled with genuine reverence.

“I will give you the oxen for burnt offerings and the threshing implements for the wood. All this I give freely, as a gift to the king.”

David shook his head. “No,” he said firmly. “I will pay you full price. I will not offer to the Lord that which costs me nothing.” Hello! Did you hear that? Those who love to give the leftovers from the ‘I don’t need this any longer’ closets, be warned.

With this, David insisted on buying the site. He knew that an offering to God must come from the heart, and he wanted it to be a true sacrifice, not a mere gesture.

The transaction was completed, and David began the preparations for building the altar.

Ornan watched with a mixture of awe and respect as the king set about his work, laying the foundation for what would soon become a sacred place of worship.

Days passed, and the altar was completed. David, with a heart full of gratitude and repentance, offered sacrifices on the altar to the Lord.

The smoke of the burnt offerings rose to the heavens, a symbol of David's devotion and a plea for divine mercy.

As the fragrant smoke mingled with the air, David felt a profound sense of peace.

He knew that his act of faithfulness was a crucial step in mending his relationship with God and restoring the favor of the Lord upon his people.

In the weeks that followed, the Lord responded with a blessing. The plague that had ravaged Israel began to recede, and the people of Jerusalem witnessed the renewal of God's grace.

Friends, David's actions reflect the sowing of seeds of obedience and faithfulness. In his youth, David was known for his devotion to God, his courage in facing Goliath, and his unwavering trust in the Lord. These youthful seeds of faith were nurtured through years of following God's commands and seeking His guidance.

In our own lives, the seeds we plant during our formative years have profound implications for our future.

When we dedicate ourselves to understanding God's Word, embracing His commands, and living out His teachings, we are planting seeds that will bear fruit in our adulthood.

These early commitments to God, will set the stage for his later decisions and actions, illustrating the principle of sowing and reaping.

The Harvest of Integrity and Faith:

The story also tells us about the harvest that follows David's actions. By purchasing the threshing floor and building an altar, David is not only making a personal sacrifice but also establishing a lasting legacy of worship.

His integrity and faithfulness continued to shape his reign and the history of Israel.

Likewise, when we sow seeds of integrity, righteousness, and dedication to God, these qualities grow and mature, influencing our character and the impact we have on others.

We learn from David's experience that the true value of the harvest is often seen in the midst of our trials and obedience.

When we remain steadfast in our commitment to God, even when the journey is tough, we position ourselves to receive the harvest of His blessings and grace.

Years later, the threshing floor of Ornan would become the site of Solomon's Temple, a grand edifice dedicated to the worship of God and the center of Israel's spiritual life.

What began as a humble threshing floor became a beacon of faith and a testament to the enduring power of obedience and sacrifice.

And so, in the quiet stillness of the evening, King David looked over the site he had consecrated, his heart full of both sorrow and hope.

He had planted a seed of faith and repentance, and it had grown into a legacy that would stand the test of time, reminding generations to come, of the importance of giving one's best to the Lord.

And today, years after David, the threshing floor of Ornan stood not only as a historical landmark, but as a powerful symbol of how our faithful actions in times of trial can yield a harvest of grace and blessings, transforming the ordinary into the extraordinary through divine providence.

So what?

As we reflect on this passage, let us consider the seeds we are currently planting. Are we sowing seeds of faith, love, and righteousness?

Are we investing in our spiritual growth and nurturing our relationship with God?

The seeds we plant today, whether in our personal lives, in our families, or in our communities, will have a significant impact on our future.

Let us be intentional about those seeds as they are sown, understanding that they will shape our future and the future of those around us.

May we, like King David, commit ourselves to building an altar of worship and obedience, ensuring that the seeds that we plant are grounded in faith and righteousness

Let us pray.

Heavenly Father,

We thank You for the lesson in 1 Chronicles and for the example of David's faithfulness. Help us to plant seeds of obedience, love, and integrity in our lives. May the seeds we sow today produce a harvest of righteousness and joy in the future.

Strengthen us to remain faithful through all trials and to trust in Your perfect timing. Guide us as we strive to live out Your Word and build a legacy that honors You.

In Jesus' name, we pray, Amen.

Chapter 19
Message: Joy in Community

Scripture: Hebrews 10:24-25

Good morning, church family! Today, we gather to explore the theme "Joy in Community."

Our scripture comes from Hebrews 10:24-25, which reminds us,

"And let us consider how we may spur one another on toward love and good deeds, not giving up meeting together, as some are in the habit of doing, but encouraging one another—and all the more as you see the Day approaching."

As we approach Christmas, a time of connection and celebration, let's deeply think about the joy we find in our community and how we can support and uplift one another on this journey.

In a world that often promotes individualism and isolation, the Scriptures remind us of the inherent joy found in fellowship with one another.

The beauty of community is rooted in our shared experiences, our collective worship, and our mutual encouragement.

The Biblical Basis for Community:

Hebrews 10:24-25 reads, "And let us consider how we may spur one another on toward love and good deeds, not giving up meeting together, as some are in the habit of doing, but encouraging one another."

These verses stress the importance of gathering as a body of believers. Our faith is not a solitary journey; it is meant to be shared.

Throughout Scripture, we see God's desire for His people to be in community.

From the early church in Acts to the gatherings of believers throughout the epistles, the message is clear: we thrive together.

When we come together, we can share our joys, bear each other's burdens, and grow in our faith collectively.

The Importance of Community:

1. Created for Connection:

From the very beginning, God designed us for relationships. In Genesis, we see that after creating Adam, God said, "It is not good for the man to be alone" (Genesis 2:18).

This speaks to our inherent need for community. We thrive in environments where we share our lives, hopes, and dreams with others.

2. Encouragement in Fellowship:

The writer of Hebrews urges us to "spur one another on." This is a call to active participation in each other's lives.

In a world that often feels isolating, Life can be challenging, and the burdens we carry can feel heavy.

We have the opportunity to create a space where encouragement abounds.

Joy in community is not merely about gathering; it's about intentionally lifting each other up, especially as we navigate challenges.

It becomes a gift we can offer that brings immense joy, and therefore, this reciprocal encouragement fosters a joyful environment where faith does flourish.

3. Sharing Hopes and Dreams:

Advent is a season of anticipation, and part of that anticipation is sharing our hopes and dreams.

When we come together as a community, we can share our desires for the future, both personally and collectively.

This sharing fosters a sense of belonging and creates an environment where joy can flourish.

Living Out Joy in Community:

1. Be Present:

One of the simplest yet most profound ways we can encourage one another is through our presence.

Whether it's attending church, joining a small group, or participating in community events, being present shows that we care.

This presence allows us to share in each other's joys and sorrows, creating bonds that deepen our relationships.

2. Listen and Validate:

Encouragement comes in many forms, and one of the most impactful is simply listening.

When someone shares their dreams or fears, taking the time to listen and validate their feelings can provide immense joy.

We all want to be heard and understood, and your attentive heart can make a world of difference.

3. Create Opportunities for Connection:

As we move through this Advent season, let's look for ways to create joy-filled moments together.

This could be through hosting gatherings, sharing meals, or engaging in service projects.

Each opportunity allows us to celebrate our community and remind one another that we are not alone on this journey.

As we prepare our hearts for Christmas, let's remember the joy that comes from being in a community.

We are called to encourage one another, sharing our hopes and dreams as we walk together.

In doing so, we reflect the love of Christ and embody the spirit of this season.

Let us pray:

Heavenly Father,

Thank You for the gift of community. Help us to encourage one another, to share in each other's joys, and to be present in one another's lives.

May our fellowship be a source of joy as we journey together toward Christmas. In Jesus' name, we pray.

Amen.

Chapter 20

Message: An unwavering woman of virtue and courage

Scripture: Exodus 1:17-20

Happy Mother's Day. Today's message is about the lives of three remarkable women of the Bible: Shiphrah & Puah from the book of Exodus, Lydia and Rhoda are from the Acts of the Apostles.

Through their faith, courage, and devotion, they have left an indelible mark on the pages of scripture, inspiring us to trust the God who has called us to a life of purpose and conviction.

Exodus 1:17-20, Shiphrah and Puah, two Hebrew midwives who defied the orders of Pharaoh and refused to kill Hebrew baby boys at birth.

Despite the threat of severe punishment, they chose to obey God rather than Pharaoh, demonstrating unwavering faith and a commitment to righteousness. Their courage in the face of adversity reminds us that even in the darkest of times, we must stand firm in our convictions and trust in the Lord's protection.

Turning to Acts 16:14-15, we meet Lydia, a wealthy businesswoman from Thyatira. Despite her status and success, Lydia remained humble and open-hearted, eagerly receiving the message of the Gospel from the apostle Paul. Her hospitality and generosity of love knew no bounds, as she welcomed Paul and his companions into her home and supported their ministry with her resources.

Finally, in Acts 12:14, we encounter Rhoda, a young servant girl in the house of Mary, the mother of John Mark. When Peter, imprisoned for preaching the Gospel, miraculously appeared at the gate, Rhoda's faith was put to the test.

Despite the disbelief of those around her, Rhoda remained steadfast in her conviction that God had answered their prayers. Her simple yet profound faith serves as a reminder that God often works in mysterious ways and that we must always trust in His timing and His plan.

Church, as we reflect upon the lives of these faithful women, let us be inspired to emulate their virtues of courage, humility, and unwavering faith.

Chapter 21
Message: The final Journey
(Passing Away from the World as We Know It)

Scripture: Psalm 23.

This morning, we will be speaking about a subject that is both profound and impossible to escape—the final journey of every human being on this earth.

Yes, it is a journey that each one of us will undertake, just like our dear sister just did, but it is also a journey that remains shrouded in mystery until the moment it arrives.

The passing away from the world as we know it, is a moment of profound significance, and it is a subject that calls for reflection, understanding, and spiritual preparation.

As we look into this topic, let us first acknowledge the natural tendency to fear the unknown, including the unknown of death.

It is a fear that has gripped humanity for centuries, and it is a fear that often leads to denial or avoidance. However, as people of Christian faith, we are called to face this reality head-on and approach it with a sense of spiritual understanding and hope.

The final journey is a transition—a passage from this earthly existence into the realm of the eternal. Just as we are born into this world with cries of life, we depart with the whisper of eternity.

It is a moment when our physical bodies, which have served us as vessels in this world, are left behind, and our souls continue on a journey that transcends time and space. How do we know this? The Bible tells me so... "That in the absence from this body is in the presence of God."

In the face of this inevitability, we find peace in the teachings of our faith. In the Bible, we are reminded that death is not the end but a new beginning— Psalm 23, one of the most cherished passages in the Bible, offers us profound insights into the final journey. Please pick your bible and open it to:

Psalm 23: (NIV)

A psalm of David.

1 The LORD is my shepherd, I lack nothing.

2 He makes me lie down in green pastures,

he leads me beside quiet waters,

3 he refreshes my soul.

He guides me along the right paths

for his name's sake.

4 Even though I walk

through the darkest valley,

I will fear no evil,

for you are with me;

your rod and your staff,

they comfort me.

5 You prepare a table before me

in the presence of my enemies.

You anoint my head with oil;

my cup overflows.

6 Surely your goodness and love will follow me

all the days of my life,

and I will dwell in the house of the LORD

forever.

It begins with these words: "The Lord is my shepherd; I shall not want" (Psalm 23:1). These words remind us that even in our final moments, we are not alone.

The Lord, our loving Shepherd, is with us every step of the way. His presence brings comfort, peace, and assurance, for we shall lack nothing when we place our trust in Him.

As we journey through life, we encounter moments of green pastures and still waters, times of tranquility and abundance.

Yet, we also navigate through the valley of the shadow of death, where fear and uncertainty can grip our hearts.

But in Psalm 23:4, we are reminded that even in the darkest valley, we need not fear, for our Shepherd is beside us, guiding and protecting us.

Let me repeat this again:

Verse 4 of Psalm 23:4 says, "Even though I walk through the valley of the shadow of death, I will fear no evil, for you are with me; your rod and your staff, they comfort me."

These words should bring us great comfort in the face of the final journey. Our Shepherd's rod symbolizes His protection, and His staff signifies His guidance.

In our moments of vulnerability, His presence provides peace and strength. Friends, the final journey is just a passage from this temporal world into the realm of eternity.

As we have just heard, Psalm 23 reminds us that it is not a solitary journey, but one undertaken in the presence of our Shepherd Himself, with His Angels leading the way.

As Christians, we believe that through faith in Jesus Christ, we have the promise of eternal life.

In John 14:2-3, Jesus Himself assured us, saying, "In my Father's house are many rooms. If it were not so, would I have told you that I go to prepare a place for you? And if I go and prepare a place for you, I will come again and will take you to myself, that where I am you may be also."

This promise reassures us that the final journey is not an end but a beginning—an entrance into the eternal dwelling prepared for us by our Savior.

You see, the final journey also invites us to reflect on the life we have lived. It prompts us to consider the impact we have had on others and the relationships we have nurtured through disciplining as commanded by the Lord.

As we stand on the threshold of eternity, we are called to examine our hearts and our souls. Have we lived a life of purpose and meaning?

Have we shown kindness and compassion to our fellow beings? Have we sought forgiveness for our shortcomings and striven for spiritual growth?

For it is in these moments of reflection that we can find peace and reassurance.

As followers of Christ, we are taught that a life lived in accordance with our spiritual values prepares us for this final journey.

I will tell you a secret today; It is a journey where our deeds and intentions will be weighed, and the sincerity of our faith will be revealed, someone say Amen.

In times of grief and loss, we often turn to our faith for comfort. We find peace in the promise of reunion with loved ones who have gone before us and with the belief that, they are in the presence of God, all suffering will have ceased.

It is a time when our faith becomes a source of strength, guiding us through the dark valley of loss toward the eternal light of hope.

May we find comfort in the words of the Psalmist: "Even though I walk through the valley of the shadow of death, I will fear no evil, for you are with me; your rod and your staff, they comfort me." (Psalm 23:4)

Friends, Let us pray for the grace to live a life of purpose and faith, so that when our final journey arrives, we may do so with hope and confidence.

Because we Know that, we are passing away from this world as we know it and entering into the embrace of our loving Father's arms in Christ Jesus.

You see, my friends; we have been assured that He has prepared a table before us in the presence of our enemies. He anointed our heads with oil, our cup overflows.

And Surely His goodness and love/mercy will follow us all the days of our lives, and we will dwell in the house of the Lord forever. Oh, Somebody say Amen.

Chapter 22
Message: Joyful Anticipation
Week 1: The Joy of Expectation

Scripture: Psalm 126:3.

As we gather to celebrate the first Sunday of Advent, we turn our hearts toward the theme "Joyful Anticipation."

Our scripture today, Psalm 126:3, reminds us, "The Lord has done great things for us, and we are filled with joy."

This verse invites us to reflect on the incredible blessings we have received and to prepare our hearts for the joy of Christ's coming.

Understanding the Context of Psalm 126:

The psalmist speaks from a place of deep gratitude. The psalm was likely written after the Israelites returned from Babylonian exile.

Their return was marked by joy and gratitude as they recognized the great things God had done for them.

This moment reflects a deep yearning fulfilled—a restoration not only of their homeland but also of their identity as God's chosen people.

Similarly, Advent invites us to remember the past, to acknowledge the great things God has done, and to look forward with hope.

As their joy was rooted in the recognition of God's faithfulness and the great things He has accomplished in their lives, it is recognized that. _

This joy is not merely a fleeting emotion; it is an amazing response to God's enduring love and grace for their people.

People of First Baptist Church, and our listening audience, do you feel the same way the Israelites felt? You see, they always had.

Joyful Expectation:

1. Recognizing God's Goodness:

So, as we enter this Advent season, we are called to reflect on the great things God has done in our own lives.

What blessings have we experienced? How has God been present in our joys and our struggles?

In moments of gratitude, we find a foundation for joyful anticipation.

2. They Anticipated the Miracle of Rescued:

Advent is our time of waiting and preparing. We anticipate the birth of Christ, the ultimate gift of love and hope.

This anticipation fills us with joy because we know that His coming transforms our lives and the world around us.

We are not just looking back to a historical event; we are preparing our hearts for an ongoing relationship with Him.

3. They Shared their Joy:

Joy is meant to be shared. Just as the Israelites proclaimed the goodness of the Lord, we too, are called to share our testimonies of God's faithfulness.

This Advent, let's encourage one another by recounting the ways God has worked in our lives.

Our stories of joy can inspire hope and anticipation in others.

Application:

As we light the first candle of Advent, let it symbolize our joyful expectation. This week, let's create space in our hearts and homes for this joy to flourish.

Here are a few practical ways to cultivate joyful anticipation:

- Reflect on Gratitude: Keep a gratitude journal during Advent. Each day, write down a blessing or a way you've seen God at work.

- Create Advent Traditions: Establish family traditions that focus on preparation and joy, such as reading scripture, singing carols, or engaging in acts of service.

- Share Your Joy: Reach out to someone this week to share how God has blessed you. This could be through a call, a note, or an invitation to coffee.

As we embark on this Advent journey, let us remember that we are filled with joy because of what the Lord has done for us.

May this season be one of joyful anticipation, as we prepare our hearts for the miracle of Christ's birth. Let's embrace the joy that comes from expectation, knowing that God's faithfulness continues to unfold in our lives.

Prayer:

Gracious God, thank You for the great things You have done for us. Fill our hearts with joy as we anticipate the celebration of Christ's birth.

Help us to recognize Your goodness and share our joy with others. May this Advent be a time of deep reflection and joyful expectation. In Jesus' name, we pray. Amen.

Conclusion & The "So What Question?

The Continuing Journey of Preaching and Faith:

As we conclude this series of sermons, we are reminded that the Christian life is an ongoing journey—one that is continually shaped and formed through the power of the Word of God.

Preaching is not a one-time event or a solitary experience, but rather a means by which we are continually called to deeper levels of understanding, commitment, and transformation.

The Enduring Relevance of Preaching:

In a world marked by complexity, uncertainty, and often despair, the Church's task of preaching the Gospel remains as urgent and necessary as ever. The themes we have explored in this series—God's nature, the power of the Cross, the Christian life, and the promise of eternal hope—are not abstract ideas, but essential truths that speak directly to the human experience.

Every sermon in this collection has sought to make these truths accessible and relevant, helping believers to see the implications of the Gospel in their everyday lives.

The act of preaching brings us back to the foundations of the faith—God's Word and His work in the world.

It serves as a reminder that we are not the authors of our own salvation or the creators of our own meaning. Instead, we are recipients of a story that began long before us and will continue long after us. This story centers on the life, death, and resurrection of Jesus Christ, and it calls each of us to participate in God's redemptive work in the world.

Living Out the Truths of Preaching:

Preaching, in its purest form, is not simply about hearing or even understanding. It is about living out the truths we proclaim. The apostle James reminds us that we are to be "doers of the word, and not hearers only" (James 1:22).

True Christian preaching does not leave us unchanged. It compels us to action, to respond to the call of Christ, and to live lives that reflect His love, justice, and holiness. As we reflect on the truths shared in this sermon series, we are called to ask ourselves:

How does the nature of God shape the way we live our lives? How does the Cross challenge our view of self, sin, and salvation? How does the Christian life call us to live differently in a world that desperately needs the light of Christ? And ultimately, how does the promise of eternal life encourage us to persevere through suffering and trials?

The Ongoing Mission of the Church:

The task of preaching is not finished. The Gospel continues to go forth, inviting all people to come and know the transforming power of Christ. The Church, as the body of Christ on earth, is called to be a community that not only hears the Word but also spreads it—proclaiming the Kingdom of God to a broken and hurting world. This is the mission of the Church: to make disciples of all nations, baptizing them and teaching them to obey all that Christ has commanded (Matthew 28:19-20).

As this collection of sermons concludes, we are reminded that preaching is not just for Sunday mornings or for those gathered in our sanctuaries. The call to preach the Gospel extends beyond the pulpit and into every believer's life. We are all called to be witnesses of Christ in the world, sharing His love and truth with those around us, making disciples, and advancing His Kingdom.

Final Encouragement:

In the end, the purpose of preaching is to bring glory to God and to lead people to a deeper, more vibrant relationship with Him. We have only begun to scratch the surface of the riches of God's Word.

As you continue on your spiritual journey, may the seeds planted by these sermons bear fruit in your life. May they inspire you to seek the Lord more earnestly, to live out your calling with greater passion, and to share the hope of Christ with a world in desperate need of His grace.

The Christian faith is not a static belief but a dynamic journey that unfolds as we walk in obedience to the call of God. May you be encouraged to continue pressing forward in your faith, grounded in the Word of God and empowered by the Holy Spirit, knowing that the best is yet to come as we await the return of our Savior and the fullness of the Kingdom of God.

About the Author

Author's profile & the purpose for writing the book:

Reverend Baffour Nkrumah-Appiah is currently the Senior Pastor at First Baptist Church of Randolph, Massachusetts, where he oversees a dynamic ministry of a congregation that is fully engaged in the Kingdom work. A church with a mission to fulfill the Apostle Paul's directive in 1 Corinthians 15: 58, which serves as a reminder that every act of service, no matter how small, contributes to a greater divine purpose. Our church members are encouraged to view their work through an eternal perspective, where their labor in the Lord is seen as part of a grander scheme that transcends temporal concerns.

In this book, "The Power and Purpose of Preaching in the Christian Faith," I emphasize the vital role that preaching plays in the life of the Church and the spiritual development of believers. The book explores the significance of preaching as a divinely ordained means of communicating God's Word to a congregation, emphasizing that it is not simply a human activity but a sacred act of proclamation. It is argued that preaching is central to the growth of the Church and the individual believer, as it serves to nourish, convict, and inspire.

This book also examines the theological foundations of preaching, asserting that it is through the preached Word that people encounter the power of the Holy Spirit. It highlights the need for preaching to be both biblically faithful and culturally relevant, balancing the truths of

Scripture with the contemporary context in which it is heard. The purpose of preaching, according to my perspective, is to bring people into a deeper relationship with God, shaping their understanding of the gospel and encouraging them to live out their faith in practical ways.

Let us Pray:

Heavenly Father,

We come before You with humble hearts, grateful for the gift of Your Word and the powerful means of preaching that You have provided. We thank You for those who faithfully proclaim Your truth, that through their words, we might encounter Your presence and be transformed by Your grace. Lord, we ask that You continue to bless the ministry of preaching, empowering preachers with wisdom, clarity, and passion. May their words be filled with Your Spirit, and may they always remain faithful to the message of the gospel.

We pray that as Your Word is preached, it will take root in our hearts, changing us from the inside out. Help us to not only hear but to live according to Your truth, that we may reflect Your love and bring glory to Your name. Equip us all to be faithful listeners and doers of Your Word, so that the power of the gospel might continue to advance in our lives and in the world. We ask this in the name of Jesus, our Savior.

Amen.

Reverend Baffour Nkrumah-Appiah (DMin. Candidate) is currently the Senior Pastor at First Baptist Church of Randolph Massachusetts, where he oversees a dynamic ministry of a congregation that is fully engaged in the Kingdom work. A church with a mission to fulfil the Apostle Paul's directive in 1 Corinthians 15: 58, which serves as a reminder that every act of service, no matter how small, contributes to a greater divine purpose. Our church members are encouraged to view their work through an eternal perspective, where their labor in the Lord is seen as part of a grander scheme that transcends temporal concerns.

In this book, "The Power and Purpose of Preaching in the Christian Faith," I emphasize the vital role that preaching plays in the life of the Church and the spiritual development of believers. The book explores the significance of preaching as a divinely ordained means of communicating God's Word to a congregation, emphasizing that it is not simply a human activity but a sacred act of proclamation.

It is argued that preaching is central to the growth of the Church and the individual believer, as it serves to nourish, convict, and inspire. This book also examines the theological foundations of preaching, asserting that it is through the preached Word that people encounter the power of the Holy Spirit.

It highlights the need for preaching to be both biblically faithful and culturally relevant, balancing the truths of Scripture with the contemporary context in which it is heard. The purpose of preaching, according to my perspective, is to bring people into a deeper relationship with God, shaping their understanding of the gospel and encouraging them to live out their faith in practical ways.

Let us Pray:

Heavenly Father,

We come before You with humble hearts, grateful for the gift of Your Word and the powerful means of preaching that You have provided. We thank You for those who faithfully proclaim Your truth, that through their words, we might encounter Your presence and be transformed by Your grace. Lord, we ask that You continue to bless the ministry of preaching, empowering preachers with wisdom, clarity, and passion.

May their words be filled with Your Spirit, and may they always remain faithful to the message of the gospel.

We pray that as Your Word is preached, it will take root in our hearts, changing us from the inside out. Help us to not only hear but to live according to Your truth, that we may reflect Your love and bring glory to Your name. Equip us all to be faithful listeners and doers of Your Word, so that the power of the gospel might continue to advance in our lives and in the world. We ask this in the name of Jesus, our Savior.

Amen.

www.ingramcontent.com/pod-product-compliance
Lightning Source LLC
LaVergne TN
LVHW050601160826
845677LV00011B/2405